Contents

Drake is one of England's great heroes.
He lived in the 16th century

He was brave and daring.
He loved action and adventure.
He risked his life many times.
He was a brilliant sailor.

In the 16th century,
Spain was a very strong power.
Spain was England's great rival.
Drake fought Spain's power
and opened up the world
to English sailors and explorers.
He helped to save England
in war with Spain.

He was the first Englishman
to sail round the world.

From his travels he made a fortune,
both for himself
and for Queen Elizabeth of England.

This is his story.

1 A Boy by the Sea

Francis Drake was born in Devon in 1544.
He was the eldest of 12 boys.
His father had been a sailor,
and later a preacher.
He worked with sailors
at the navy base near Chatham.
So Francis grew up with the sea,
ships and sailors.

He spent a lot of time on the ships.
He learned about tides and winds and sails.
He was small for his age,
but he could move quickly on deck.
He did not go to school,
but he learned to read and write from his father.
As soon as he could,
Francis became a boy sailor.

Sir Francis Drake

When he was about ten
he worked on a ship.
He sailed up and down the coast.
Sometimes they crossed the Channel
to French ports.
Francis learned a lot about
how to handle ships.
They had to take food to London;
butter, cheese and fish.
Later he made trips to the ports of Holland.
All the time he learned more skills.

When he was about 17,
his employer died.
Francis worked for a few more years
in coast trade.
But he wanted adventure.
He wanted to try the open seas.
He hoped to find treasure and make his fortune.
He went to work for his cousin,
John Hawkins.

2 The New World

John Hawkins made money from slaves.
He bought slaves in Africa
and sold them in America.
At this time Spain claimed all of America.
The King of Spain said that
America had been found by the Spanish.
The 'New World' belonged to them.
In the New World
there was much silver and gold.
Men could make a fortune
by trading in the New World.
John Hawkins was trying to break into this trade.
The Spanish wanted to keep English sailors out.

Francis Drake went on his first ocean voyage
in 1566.
It was a trip to Africa
and then to the Caribbean.

Drake had to learn new skills.
He had to learn to sail the open seas.
He had to learn about sailing
in storms and heavy winds.
He had to live at sea for months at a time.
He also learned about the Spanish.
They saw the English as their rivals.
They often attacked the English ships.
Drake made up his mind
to challenge Spain in the New World.

Drake and Hawkins were attacked
on a trip to the Gulf of Mexico.
They lost men and ships.
They started their own wars with Spain.
If they could not trade,
then they would take what they could
from the Spanish.
They became pirates.

3 Spanish Treasure

Drake wanted Spain's gold and silver.
Most of it came from Peru.
It was taken by mules to a port in Panama.
From there it was loaded onto ships.
Then it went across the Atlantic to Spain.

Drake found out all he could about the trade.
He watched the port in Panama.
He checked the size of Spain's fleet.

The next year, he went back.
Drake and his men attacked the port.
They broke into the treasure house.
It belonged to the King of Spain.
But they were out of luck:
the treasure house was empty.

Drake was shot in the leg
and lost a lot of blood.
His men took him back to the ship.
But he was not ready to go home.
He did not have the gold and silver.

Drake explored the coast
and the hot jungle.
He saw the Pacific Ocean for the first time –
he said that one day, he wanted to sail there.

He waited for another mule train
to come down to the port.
This time, Drake and his men
stopped the mules and took all the silver.
There were 190 mules
each carrying 135kg of silver.
Drake and his men took all they could carry,
and buried the rest.
They took all the gold too.
There was so much of it,
they did not have room on the ship.
Bags of sand had been used as ballast.
Drake threw them out.
He used gold and silver instead.

4 Drake Lies Low

Drake came back to Devon in 1573.
He had won a fortune from the Spanish.
He had made his name
as a great sailor.
He was known as a daring pirate.

He had been away from England for a year.
Things had changed.
Queen Elizabeth was making peace with Spain.
It was not a good time for Drake to turn up
with stolen Spanish treasure.
He was warned
to keep out of the way.
For two years
nothing was heard of him.

Drake had gone to Ireland.
He was helping to deal with Irish rebels.

But Drake could not forget the Pacific Ocean.
He longed to go back there.

In 1577 he had the chance.

The plan was to find new lands
and new trade for England.
A group of important people would
put up the money.
One of them was Queen Elizabeth.
Some people say
she had given Drake a secret order –
to attack Spain's ships.
No one knows if that was true.
But she must have known
that Drake would try!

5 Around the World

Drake set sail in December 1577.
He did not see England again
until September 1580.
In those years
he sailed right round the world.
This had been done only once before;
by Magellan.

Drake took five ships and 164 men with him.
His own ship was called *The Pelican*.
It was the only one to return home.
By then it had a new name: *The Golden Hind*.

Drake had many adventures on this voyage.

They sailed for months without seeing land.
They saw strange birds and fish.
Some of the crew were afraid.

Drake travelled to many countries

One of them spoke out against Drake.
It was Thomas Doughty.
He tried to turn the men against Drake.
Drake had to show
that he was a strong leader.
He put Doughty on trial.
Then he had him killed.

Drake knew that when men were at sea,
they had to trust their captain.
He also said that at sea
all men should do the same jobs.
They should be treated in the same way.
Their class did not matter.

So Drake won the respect of his men.
They trusted him in times of danger.
There were bad storms
at the tip of South America.
One ship was lost.
But Drake went on.
He gave his ship a new name, *The Golden Hind*,
and hoped for better luck.

They met up with
a big Spanish treasure ship.
Drake's men boarded the ship
and took gold, silver, jewels and sugar.

Drake landed on the coast of California.
He left a brass plate with his name on it.
It said Drake claimed the land for England.

He took the first English ship
into the Pacific Ocean.
Drake went to many islands in the Pacific.
He bought spices.
They were very valuable at home.

Then Drake went on
to sail round the coast of Africa.
From there he made his way
back to England.

The Golden Hind came into Plymouth
on 26 September 1580.
They had been away for almost three years.

6 Fame and Riches

Drake was a hero in England.
But he did not know
how the Queen would treat him.
He had made fools of the Spanish.
The King of Spain was sure to ask Drake
to give back the money he had stolen.

The King of Spain did not know
Queen Elizabeth had backed Drake's voyage.
She had made a lot of money out of it.
But in public
she might have to punish Drake.
His friends joked that he would go to prison.
But the Queen told Drake to come and see her.
He took some of the treasure with him.
Elizabeth was pleased.
She let Drake keep £10,000 for himself.
She kept over £300,000!

Then later, she visited him
on board his ship *The Golden Hind.*
Drake had a feast ready.
The Queen came with a sword.
It was to cut off his head
as the King of Spain wanted.
Instead, the Queen used the sword
to make him a knight.
He was now Sir Francis Drake.

He was also given lands
and a house in Devon.
Earlier in 1569,
he had found time between trips
to get married in Devon to Mary Newman.
But he had never spent long with her
before he was off on his next trip!

The people of Plymouth
voted for him to be their Mayor.
He also became an MP.
Over the next few years,
he worked for the Queen.

Drake had won fame and riches.
But his days of adventure
were not over.

Francis Drake is knighted by Queen Elizabeth

7 War with Spain

In the 1580s Spain and England drifted to war.
Spain and England were rivals
and England thought that Spain
had too much power
both in Europe and in the New World.

England wanted to challenge that power.
Drake's plan was
to take away their gold and silver.

So there were more attacks
and raids on Spanish ships.
Each one was more daring than the last.

The King of Spain began to prepare
a great fleet of ships to invade England.

But Drake was not afraid to risk his own life.

He took ships to Spain itself.
He sailed into the port of Cadiz,
where the war ships were getting ready.
He destroyed many of the ships.
He took many of their supplies.
Drake caught them by surprise.
He was able to sail away
before they could do anything.

Drake's raid on Cadiz
delayed the attack on England.
But the Spanish fleet (armada)
set sail in July 1588.
The Spanish sent 132 ships.
As they came into the Channel,
it was hard to attack them.
The fleet was in a half moon shape.
The strong ships were on the outside
so it would be hard to break up the group.

The English fleet was led by Lord Howard.
Drake's ship was called *Revenge*.
There were other good sailors
in the English fleet.
They were all keen to fight the Spanish
and stop them landing on English soil.

A Spanish captain surrenders to Sir Francis Drake

The English ships chased the Spanish,
and attacked them in the rear.
But they could not break up the fleet.
It seemed to be stalemate.

Then the English came up with a good plan.
It may well have been Drake's idea.

They packed ships with dry wood and tar.
Then they set fire to them
and sent them into the Spanish fleet.
There was panic and the Spanish ships
broke up their group.
It was now easy to attack them.

A strong wind blew the Armada north.
Soon the Spanish were lost in the North Sea.
They could not land in England.
They could not get back home.
They had to sail north around Britain.
Many of their ships were lost
or wrecked in Scotland and Ireland.
The Armada had failed.

The leading English sailors were
Hawkins, Drake and Howard.
All were rivals,
all wanted to be heroes.
They fell out among themselves.

But the war was not over.
There was a plan
to send an English armada to Spain.
The plan was to destroy Spain's fleet
so it would never be a danger again.
Drake was to lead the English armada.

But the plan did not work.
This time the winds were against the English
and scattered their ships.
Many of the men were ill and many died.
Some of the sailors got drunk
on Spanish wine.

When Drake came home this time,
people said he had failed.
His rivals were glad
to see him out of favour.

8 The Last Voyage

The war with Spain dragged on for many years.
Drake still had a big part to play.
He went back to being a pirate again.
He stole Spanish treasure in the New World.

In 1595 he went to the West Indies
with his cousin, Hawkins.
It was to be the last time for both of them.
Again they argued.
They could not seem to work well together.

Then the English sailors went down with fever.
Men died like flies.
When Drake fell ill,
Hawkins had already died.
Drake was ill in his cabin for days.
He died on 28 January 1596.
His body was put into a lead coffin
and it was sunk in the sea.
Two ships from his fleet were sunk with him.
The sea, where Drake had first made his name,
was now his grave.

9 Drake's Drum

Drake was buried at sea,
to the sound of his own drum.
It was the drum that had been used
to call his sailors to action.
The drum was taken back to England.

There is a legend that says,
when England is in danger,
Drake's drum will beat.
He will know that England needs him
and he will come back!